Frack

Tales from Hunter Hollow

Annie-Laurie Hunter

Copyright © 2015 Annie-Laurie Hunter

All rights reserved.

ISBN: 1507770480
ISBN-13: 978-1507770481

This book is dedicated to all the people who work tirelessly to care for animals in need and to all the animals, especially the bunnies that never find a "furever" home.

Annie-Laurie Hunter

This book is a compilation of stories and conversations of the bunnies that have spent some time at Hunter Hollow. All domestic bunnies need homes with families to care for them and provide the love and attention they deserve. Sometimes bunnies find themselves without a home. Some of them arrive here. Before leaving here the bunnies are spayed or neutered and demonstrate good social skills.

Caring for the bunnies during this transitional time has become a powerful experience in caring and letting go. I hope that in reading this book you will share with me the delight, the sorrow, and the hope of the bunnies that for a time call Hunter Hollow home.

Annie-Laurie Hunter

Frick and Frack were worried this morning.
Frack: Are we going to get killed?
Me: No, why?
Frick: We've been here longest and we heard that if animals don't get adopted fast enough they get killed.
Me: That doesn't happen here. You will be here until there is room at the shelter and you will stay there until you find a family. We don't kill bunnies because they haven't found a family.
Frack: What about Buttons? Buttons keeps biting.
Me: Either Buttons will learn to trust people and be able to have a family or Buttons will live out her life here.
Frick: Where are you going to put everyone?
Me: I'm working on it. We will do some shifting around and squeeze you all in. You won't have a playroom, but you will have your lives and where there is life, there is hope.
Frack: Um, Mom, thanks for having us and um, can we have some carrot juice?

The Cauliflower Chronicles part 1

Day 1:

My family just brought me to this noisy place. There are dogs barking all around me. I am in a little cage and there is food and a water bottle but I don't like it here. I want to get out of this cage. Biting the bars doesn't seem to help. Maybe I'll try the carrot.

Day 2:

My family hasn't come back. A nice person picked me up and held me. She said I was sweet. She is going to find me a new place to live. My family doesn't want me anymore because I am growing too big. I want to run around. I hate this cage and I wish the dogs would stop all that noise.

Day 3:

No one came today to hold me or let me run around. I tried to dig my way out of the cage through the litter pan. The litter pan has a bottom. I tried hard to get through it but no luck. I will try again later. Maybe I'll have some hay.

Day 4:

I got fresh water and food. I'm bored. The dogs won't be quiet.

Day 5:

Someone brought more food and water. It is just the same boring food as yesterday. I still can't dig through the litter box. But I can't hear the dogs while I am digging. Maybe I will dig some more.

Day 6:

I saw the doctor today. He said if I am still here on Monday I am going to go to sleep. I don't really understand--I sleep every day for a while. What is a Monday? Maybe if I eat the carrot I will figure it out.

Bunnies!

I just finished loading in 2 bales of hay, 50 pounds of bunny chow, a case and a half of lettuce and a few bunches of bananas and Skyler asks, "Did you get any carrots?"

"Not today."

And I heard him grumble to Emily, "She never gets us anything good to eat."

As I was serving dinner tonight I explained to my crew that four of them are going in for alterations tomorrow. Frick and Frack were excited: Frack wants longer ears and Frick is hoping for a tail plumping- apparently this is the latest fashion. Big Brown said his coat fits just fine and Charlie suggested that he have his ears lopped. Akita told them they were all imbeciles and that that wasn't what I meant by alterations. He has been there, done that, and will never be quite the same.

Annie-Laurie Hunter

I was just feeding the crew dinner and Frack asked, "Mom, how come Frick and I are sisters and our fur looks the same but feels different?"
So, I responded, "It is because of your genes."
And Frick starts laughing, "Mom, you are so silly! We have fur coats, we don't wear pants."

Frick: Mom, why do you clean our cage and give us new litter every week?
Me: So you won't be stinky bunnies.
Frack: What do you do with the old litter?
Me: People who garden come and get the litter so they can grow vegetables.
Frick: Mom, that is the silliest story you have ever told us; vegetables grow from seeds, not poops.

Frick: Mom? How come after you clean out our cage we only have water and hay for a few hours?

Me: Why do you think that is?

Frick: I think it is to make sure we eat enough hay.

Frack: I think it is because you have worked so hard cleaning all the cages that you forget about the food dishes.

Me: Those are both interesting reasons, but actually, it is just because we don't have enough dishes to do a complete swap and so you need to wait for the dishes to be run through the dishwasher.

Frick looked at Frack: Wow. That was a boring reason.

Frick: Mom, we were in the library and we found a book about clicker training.

Me: Do you want to learn clicker training?

Frack: Yeah, it looks really great.

Me: We can do clicker training. What do you want to be clicker-trained to do?

Frick: We want to click the clicker and have you give us a treat.

The Cauliflower Chronicles: part 2

Day 7:

The nice person came back. She packed me in a little box and carried me away from the barking dogs. It was cold and quiet and then warm as she put my box into a big box. The big box is purring and moving. It stopped moving and I was in the cold and then in the warm and now I am in a bigger cage and it is quiet. I have a new litter box and I smell other bunnies. I don't see them but I smell them. The nice person is bringing me red romaine. Oh, I like red romaine. And here is a carrot. And look at the hay all soft and green. I could just click my heels, I am so happy.

Day 8:

The nice person let me run all around a big room. I showed her I was happy by jumping in the air and peeing at the same time. I practiced it at the old family's house. It takes practice to jump in the air and let go right when you are at the highest point in the jump. And it needs to be a high jump. I like to see how high I can jump. I bet I can jump higher than anyone else. The nice person put me back in my new cage.

Day 9:

The nice person packed me in the little box and took me through the cold to the purring box with the talking people I can't see. She said I am going to a foster home. She wants me to be happy and to grow as big as I am supposed to grow and to learn all my bunny lessons and to find a forever home. Then the purring box stopped and she took me into the cold and then I got into another box. The nice lady talked to another person for a while and then the new lady got into the purring box and people started talking and the purring box started moving and I fell asleep. Now I am in a new cage and I have new hay and a new carrot and a new water bottle and new bunny chow and I really don't know what is going on.

Frick: Mom, can we watch Mittens on TV?
Me: Sure...
Frack: How come he is going to be on TV?
Me: He is going to tell everyone that there are bunnies at the shelter that need homes.
Frick: We could tell people that; how come we didn't get to go on TV and tell people, Mom?
Me: Well, they wanted a bunny that would sit quietly on someone's lap.
Frick and Frack looked at each other: Good thing they've got Mittens...

Charlie was quieter than usual today

Me: Charlie, are you okay?

Charlie: I heard about speech not being free and I don't have a very big allowance so I wanted to be frugal about using it.

Me: You heard about what happened in France?

Charlie: It was on the news and Je suis Charlie?

Me: Yes, you are Charlie, but you live in the U. S. People have fought long and hard to ensure that we have free speech.

Charlie: I don't have to use up my allowance to talk?

Me: No, Charlie, you can talk as much as you want about whatever you want. But Charlie, I think you should know that where people don't have free speech, they don't pay with their allowances; they pay with their lives.

Charlie: I am glad I live here. That price is a lot bigger than my allowance.

Hershey asked a question this morning at breakfast:

I heard you talking with Charlie about free speech, but now I'm confused. If we have free speech then is what people say priceless or worthless?

The Cauliflower Chronicles: part 3

Day 10:

She brought me a mushy thing this morning that smelled funny. I wasn't going to taste it but she said it was good and put some on my lip. It is called a banana. Well, if that is any indication of where I am, I want to stay here. Banana, now that is something worth waking up for. She picked me up and held me and told me that she is Annie-Laurie. She keeps saying Cauliflower. She thinks I am a cauliflower! I am a bunny and she is calling me Cauliflower. Doesn't she know that I am a bunny, not a cauliflower? What kind of creature confuses a bunny with a cauliflower? And she controls the cage door. There are going to have to be a few changes around here. I am staying as long as there is banana but I am going to have to show her that if she thinks I am a cauliflower, she has no right to be in charge of who is in cages and who opens the doors.

Day 11:

No bananas today. She brought little round green things instead. Little round green things are good. Everything here is tasty. She let me out of the cage. Now I know that the table leg is tasty and the books in the book case are tasty. The carpet is a little tough. I will have to work on the carpet. I tried jumping up and peeing but there isn't enough room to get good height. I had to just helicopter in place. She still thinks I am a cauliflower but I like it when she holds me and rubs my ears.

Day 12:

I met some new bunnies today. There is a mean boy bunny named Oblio. He growled at me and told me I should leave. There is a big girl bunny named Nutmeg. She tried to bite me but the cage was in the way so she couldn't get me. I tried to bite her back but the cage was in the way for me, too. Then Annie-Laurie came in and told them that if they were going to be mean, they would have to leave. Now I am alone in the room in my little cage and I don't like being in my cage and I don't like being alone. I want to go find Nutmeg and bite her on the butt. I will have to settle for hay.

Day 13:

Annie-Laurie put a gate in the doorway to the room before letting me out of the cage. Nutmeg came to the gate and called me names so I jumped over the gate and bit her. Annie-Laurie pulled me off her and picked me up and put me back in my cage. Then she held Nutmeg. I wish she held me.

Day 14:

Here is better than the noisy place and the food is great but I feel all jittery. I keep biting the bars so Annie-Laurie will let me get out of the cage. I can't stand being in the little space. When Annie-Laurie lets me out I run all around the room and I try to pee everywhere so that it will be mine. Annie-Laurie doesn't like it when I pee anywhere but my litter box but I don't mind. I sort of like the attention I get when she calls me, even if she calls me Cauliflower.

Day 15:

Annie-Laurie put up a second gate on top of the first gate and let me out of the cage. I tried to jump over but I can only get to half way up the second gate. I am stuck in this room. Nutmeg came to the door and made rude comments. I tried to bite her but she moved away. I spent the day exploring my room. There are table legs and chair legs and I can jump onto the chair and then onto the table and then onto the shelves and I can taste all the books. I can look out the window and I can eat the window sill and I can hop on the sewing table and oops. Annie-Laurie said bunnies don't belong on the sewing table. I am stuck in my cage again. I hate this cage. I wish I could just bite through the bars and escape!!!

Day 16:

I tried to escape again today but I still can't jump over 2 gates. So I climbed all over the room. Annie-Laurie says that I am not a cat. Nutmeg and Oblio still say mean things to me and call me names. I keep trying to bite them. The gates are still in the way.

Day 17:

Annie-Laurie said we are going to try something new today. She said that I am clearly an angry little bunny and that I hate to be cooped up, so we are going outside. I have seen outside. It's what's out the window. She took me to a pen with a hutch. I can be in the hutch or I can climb down a step and be in the pen. I can hop and there is this soft fringy green stuff that tastes great. I can poop on the green stuff and pee on the green stuff and hop and rest and hop and hop and there is Nutmeg. She is outside too. She is on the other side of my pen wall. I am going to get her. I will figure a way out of here and I will get her. There isn't a hole along the base of the pen. But I can dig. Yeah, I will dig a tunnel. I will get Nutmeg.

Day 18:

I spent all day trying to dig a tunnel. I was exhausted last night. I didn't really mind when Annie-Laurie tucked me into my cage with fresh lettuce and carrots and new kibble and told me that it was time for little bunnies to go to sleep. Today I went out to the pen again but my tunnel wasn't there. I don't know what happened. It was there when I went to my cage last night but it was gone this morning. Is this a magic hutch? Nutmeg came by and asked what was wrong. I told her my tunnel was gone. She said that happens everywhere in the whole yard. We dig and dig but the holes disappear overnight. She wants to stay outside one night to see how they get filled in. I want to do that too.

Frick: Mom, can we chew on this book?
Me: No, that's a good astronomy book; why would you want to chew it up?
Frack: It's really stupid. It said that the sun is closest to the earth in the winter.
Frick: And we know that isn't true because the sun is hot and it's really cold out.
Me: Did you read the next paragraph?
Frack: No, we just decided they were stupid so we stopped reading.

Frick: Mom, we read the next paragraph.
Me: What did you learn?
Frack: Stuff is more complicated than we thought.

Frack: Mom, we keep reading the next paragraph but we can't learn all this star stuff.

Me: You don't need to learn all that star stuff. No one can learn everything. That's why we have experts.

Frick: So what should we do?

Me: You should learn enough to be able ask good questions and when you need to know more you can ask an expert.

Frick: Can we be experts?

Me: If you study something long and hard you can. What would you like to be experts at?

Frick and Frack looked at each other and said in unison, "Hay! We want to be experts in hay!"

Frick: Mom we have been doing our hay research.

Me: What have you found out?

Frack: We like second cut Timothy better than first cut Timothy.

Me: Why is that?

Frick: It is softer and fluffier and has nice tasty pieces in it.

Me: So what should we do with this new found knowledge?

Frack: Buy more second cut! This stuff is good.

I have the most wonderful bunnies!! They just informed me that for Mother's Day they are all going out to play in the back yard and let me clean all of their cages and the garage.

Annie-Laurie Hunter

Letters from Daisy

Daisy was abandoned and rescued in the spring of 2009. She had lost vision in one eye and the ophthalmologist determined that, other than medication, nothing could be done for it. She was spayed and after she healed she moved east and was adopted. Unfortunately, the adoption did not work out. Daisy became very fond of her foster mom. When her foster mom had hip replacement surgery, Daisy returned to Hunter Hollow. She wrote to her foster mom every few days. These are her e-mails.

Hi Mom,

I just wanted you to know that I am very happy here. I made friends with Otis and Abbey. We are all together in a big corral. We have carpets and tunnels and litter boxes and my hedgehog and toys are here and so is a penguin. We have lots of food and hay and water. Cauliflower comes to talk to us but she is a bully so she can't come in the corral. Abbey and Otis and I play tag and race. It is lots of fun. Then we get tired out and go to sleep. Annie-Laurie said that if we behave ourselves and get along we can be together in a big place instead of alone in little spaces. Big is more fun. We can really run.

Now you can go get new hips and not worry about

me while you heal. I am very happy here. But if I don't get adopted, I want to come home when you are ready for me.

Yours always,

Daisy

Hi Mom,

Annie-Laurie said you might be out of the hospital and I could send you a get well message. I hope you are feeling better. If I was there I would lick you so you would feel better. I am having fun here. I like Otis. He is also blind in one of his eyes. We sleep together after I have finished chasing him and Abbey all around the pen. We go through the tunnels and over the platforms and jump from Carpet Island to Carpet Island. It is great fun and lots of exercise. Abbey is fun to chase. We don't fight at all; I just like to chase her.

Over the weekend Annie-Laurie built a gate for the enclosure so that her neighbor, who is going to take care of us for Thanksgiving, can get in and out easily. We tested it out. We all escaped from the enclosure and went hopping all over the basement for a day. It was so much fun!!! Annie-Laurie fixed the gate and then she tricked us and when we all were back the enclosure, she closed the door and we haven't been able to escape since. Don't worry; I am working on another plan.

Daisy Dewdrop

Hi Mom,

I am glad you are home and recouping but I am very sad to hear about Angelhare Pasta. It's very sad that she needed to go on to the Rainbow Bridge when you weren't able to be with her. Have I met Scooby Doo? Do I like him? So I guess I can't bring Otis home with me, huh? I was going to try to sneak him home with me. Guess I shouldn't do that if I have an arranged wedding with Scooby Doo coming up. Oh, well, I will explain to him that we are just friends.

So how is the hip? I was wondering, did you get one new one or two? Can you hop yet?

Daisy Dewdrop

Hi Mom,

I swear I haven't bonded with Otis; we are just companions right now. That is why Annie-Laurie put the 3 of us together. She didn't want anyone to get lonely or to actually bond. Maybe Abbey could bond with Scooby Doo. She likes other bunnies. Oh, wait, if I brought Abbey and Otis home with me you would have 10 bunnies.

You don't really want 10 bunnies, do you?

Daisy

Hi Mom,

We escaped again and then we cooperated with each other to stay out longer. Otis, Abbey and I agreed to not all go into the enclosure at the same time. We figured out that Annie-Laurie won't close the gate if one of us is outside. It worked great!! We got to stay out all day yesterday and last night.

Then she tricked us again. We were playing follow the leader this morning and she brought our breakfast and we all followed Otis to the food dish.

Drats! Now we are in the enclosure again with nothing to do except play with our 3 tunnels and 2 platforms and carpets squares and food and hay and stuffed animals and each other.

I hope you are healing well.

Daisy

Hi Mom,

Yesterday Annie-Laurie made up for locking us in our tiny 50 sq. ft. enclosure. She brought us leaves!!! Two whole rakes full of dry leaves for us to play in and eat. Well, of course we jumped through them and nibbled them and rustled them and even tried napping in them. It was almost like being outside, but warmer. Then we had carrots. We don't get carrots often here because, well, I hope they don't hear me say this, but Annie-Laurie says that Otis and Abbey are trying to change species; oink oink, if you know what I mean.

Don't worry, I get plenty to eat: you would never know that she is trying to have them lose some pudge. I am helping them. My job is to chase Abbey and to run from Otis. That is how they get their exercise and Annie-Laurie says that is the best way for them to get into shape. Bunny tag is the best game ever. Will I get to play it when I marry Scooby Doo?

I am glad you are picking up speed. You know we tell our kits, "You have to walk before you can hop".

Hi Mom,

Are you healed yet? Annie-Laurie says to settle down. She said you can't be healed yet and it will take at least as long as it takes to have 2 litters of bunnies for you to be all better. Well, I am hoping you are better soon. How is Scooby-doo? Is his back end working yet? If you show him my picture, will that help?

Annie-Laurie tried starving us tonight. She didn't feed us until just a little bit ago. Since breakfast we've gone with nothing to eat except hay and bunny chow and leaves and water. We were all three of us laying together with spots forming before our working eyes we were so hungry. We barely had the strength to clamber to the food dish and begin ravaging the romaine. Life is tough when you are a bunny.

Abbey and I have been spending some time hanging out and talking. I like Abbey. Did you know that she lived here before too? She said she likes it better here than anywhere else she has ever lived. I like it at your house. Here is okay, but I am looking forward to coming home and snuggling with you.

Hi Mom,

I have bad news. Annie-Laurie has us really trapped!! We haven't been able to escape for more than a week now. We have tried everything short of making a bunnypult. We have been working on plans for the bunnypult and we have a fulcrum but alas, no lever..... I don't think a refrigerator raid is going to happen.

Maybe she will have mercy on us and give us time off for good behavior. Or maybe we will wait for the old lady taking care of us next week and we will scatter. She will never be able to catch us. We will be free for days!!!

Please tell Scooby Doo that I hope his back end is working better. I hate the yucky paste. Didn't you people go to kindergarten and get told not to eat the paste? Just because you can't eat it doesn't mean you should feed it to the bunny. Annie-Laurie says it is white and will keep my coat pretty white so I have been reluctantly eating it. It will keep my coat white, won't it?

Maybe you should give the walker to Scooby Doo now that you don't need it anymore. Just a thought.

I am sending you hugs and snuggles.

Daisy Dewdrop

Hi Mom,

I think I am going through mitosis. Annie-Laurie was brushing me today and she said I have enough fur for a whole other bunny. I know I am not pregnant because I had a little operation last spring so I must be going through mitosis. I will let you know how it works out.

We don't have our enclosure anymore. Instead of keeping us in, Annie-Laurie is keeping us out. Now we have the whole basement except for a few areas. She said she doesn't want her neighbor to have to worry about keeping us in our enclosure. She knows that we would escape so she just is letting us run around on our best behavior. She said we have to stay in the basement and Cauliflower is not allowed to visit while she is gone. So far we have explored under the work bench and behind the furnace. There is a tunnel behind the furnace. Now we have four tunnels to run through. This is a fun basement.

Yesterday Annie-Laurie brought us fresh hay and oats. Life is good!! I heard that we are having banana for breakfast tomorrow and that pears are on the menu for one day while she is gone. She said we have to behave ourselves or the sitter will not give us pears. I met her. She seems pretty nice and I am sure that I can outrun her but I don't think I will chance not having pears.

Annie-Laurie won't be home until Saturday and I am not allowed on the computer without her being here so I can't write again until she comes home. I hope you have a Hoppy Thanksgiving. This Thanksgiving I am going to be thankful that since I can't be with you, I am here with my friends.

Oh, I am not Canadian am I? Annie-Laurie keeps calling me Daisy Do-Right. I thought I was American.

Daisy

Hi Mom,

Annie-Laurie just told me about Scooby-Doo. I told Abbey and Otis and we decided to hold a memorial for him tonight at dusk. None of us actually knew him but I am going to tell Abbey and Otis about you and what you said about him and we are going to think warm thoughts to you. I guess sometimes that when the hop is gone it is time to go.

I am glad that I can still come to live with you. I am going to be even gladder when Annie-Laurie hands out our punishments. We sort of got carried away while she was gone. Ooops, or should I say poops. I think we are going to be back in the enclosure for a while. It was fun while it lasted. Maybe next time we should remember that potties are still potties even though the room is bigger.

Yours in sadness and contrition,

Daisy

Hi Mom,

Otis and I are surviving punishment. We have been put in the enclosure. Annie-Laurie has not been holding back on the oats. Abbey was in the enclosure too but I kept biting her butt so Annie-Laurie took her out. I don't want Abbey to get near Otis. I like Otis and well, Mom, I want to get married. But Annie-Laurie said that I am supposed to go back to your house and she doesn't think that Otis is part of the plan. She said that she had the three of us together to prevent this problem. Now, she said that we need to make a decision.

When I come back to your house, am I getting adopted or am I a forever bunny? Can Otis come with me?

Annie-Laurie said that I am not to pressure you. If Otis is not in your picture, she is going to re-arrange the living arrangements so that Otis and I aren't together. But, mom, I really like Otis.

Daisy

Oh Mom,

Annie-Laurie just showed me the good news. I am so happy; I could just binky all over the room! Wait till I tell Otis that we can get married! I will have Annie-Laurie take our wedding pictures and I will be sure to send you some. Do you think she will bake carrot cake for the reception? I think I will wear my white fur coat, and Otis can wear his brown and white fur coat. I am so excited!

Maybe Annie-Laurie can send out our wedding announcements. Oh, I am just so delighted. Wait till you meet him. He is just the nicest boy bunny. He pays lots of attention to me and is always making sure I am feeling loved. We sit and talk and he just has the nicest things to say about everything.

I think we will call our enclosure the honeymoon suite.

Thanks mom.

Daisy

Hi Mom,

Since Otis is a Dutch bunny, we followed the Pennsylvania Dutch custom of a Wednesday wedding. It was a very nice ceremony. Annie-Laurie took pictures so I could share the event with you. We decided to write and say our own vows.

Otis to Me:

My Dearest Daisy, you are more beautiful than the flower you are named for. A field of daisies could not outshine you on even the most beautiful summer day. My life began when I met you. You are my morning and my evening, my reason for being. If you will have me for your bonded partner I will spend every day for the rest of my life ensuring your happiness.

Me to Otis:

My Dearest Otis, when I came to stay here for a few months I had no idea how my life would change. I never thought that there would be a bunny as sweet and caring and devoted as you. I was to be with another and although I am sad for the reason that was not to be, I am so happy that I am free to give you all the love that I feel for the rest of my life.

Then we kissed. And Annie-Laurie took out pictures and we hoped off the dais and went to the reception. Our first hop was to "You Are the Apple of My Eye" It was a very nice ceremony. Now we are bonded.

Annie-Laurie talked to us about making this bonding work in the long run. We both assured her that we would turn our blind eye on each other's faults.

It has been a busy day but I wanted to share it with you.

Your Dearest Daisy

Daisy and her new husbun Otis returned to living with their long term foster mother. They were later adopted together.

Frick: Mom, Hershey said that we are a couple of dumb bunnies.

Me: I wouldn't call you dumb bunnies.

Frack: See Hershey? We are not dumb bunnies.

Hershey: What would you call them?

Me: Although they may be lacking in information and comprehension on a wide variety of topics, I am going to call them Frick and Frack and I strongly suggest you do too.

Hershey was smart enough to turn away before he snickered.

Me: The question has come up about what constitutes a crazy bunny lady and what the qualifications are for it. And it was suggested that I ask you two.

Frick: Do we get chamomile tea if we get it right?

Frack: Well, I just started reading the DSM-V but I think anyone who thinks you should ask a couple of little bunnies about a psychiatric diagnosis must have a classification in here somewhere.

Frick: I think you just wrecked our chance of getting chamomile tea.

Frick: Mom, we haven't found a family yet.

Frack: How come, Mom?

Me: Perhaps there just isn't yet a family that has realized what great bunnies you are.

Frick: How do we make them realize?

Me: You work on your cuteness lessons and your cage neatness.

Frack: We're doing that but it hasn't worked.

Me: You can only do what's in your control. Trying to control the rest of the world will just make you very unhappy and frustrated bunnies.

Frick: Yeah, well, it isn't easy.

Frack: We can control hay munching and arranging: let's move this hay to over there.

Frick: Mom, are you worried about the Department of Labor coming here?

Me: Why would I be worried about the Department of Labor?

Frack: We're reading this book about the history of work in America and about child labor laws.

Me: That isn't typical bunny material...but, okay. What does it have to do with me?

Frick: You said this is a regular poop factory.

Frack: And you have little bunnies working here...

Annie-Laurie Hunter

Hunter Hollow Bunny Bed and Breakfast

Once in a while, Hunter Hollow becomes a Bed and Breakfast for traveling bunnies. As with all good Bed and Breakfasts, special accommodations are made to ensure the comfort of the travelers.
In the fall of 2009 a group of bunnies and guinea pigs from an over-crowded shelter moved west to a shelter that could accommodate them. Because of travel logistics, the bunnies and guinea pigs stopped at the Hunter Hollow Bunny Bed and Breakfast for one night.

Itinerary for the Fall Foliage Tour Group

Check-in is 3:00 pm.

    Two large cabins for the bunnies and one cabin for the guinea pigs will be ready upon their arrival. Snacks and drinks will be available in all cabins.

    The salad buffet is scheduled for 7:00pm followed by a cello concert for evening entertainment before bed.

A fruit platter will be served on Saturday

morning followed by quiet relaxation before continuing the intra-state Fall Foliage tour.

We at Hunter Hollow Bunny Bed and Breakfast look forward to meeting the Fall Foliage tour group and ensuring their travel is as stress-free as possible.

A large bunny transport was arranged in the fall of 2008 to move some bunnies east as far as Boston and some south to southern Pennsylvania. These abused bunnies had been seized and now needed new homes. The bunnies bound for Pennsylvania spent a week at the Hunter Hollow Bunny Bed and Breakfast.

Itinerary

Saturday 10:00am: get in a box and hop in a car.

Saturday 3:30pm: get out of the damned box!!!

Bunny Orientation at the Hunter Hollow Bunny Bed and Breakfast

Each bunny has been booked into a single room with private bathroom accommodations. Room service will be provided, including a continental breakfast and vegetarian cuisine for dinner. Vegetarian snacks are available upon demand and of course, there is always the finest Skaneateles Lake water available to quench one's thirst.

The days are very structured with a variety of activities to help the traveling bunnies make the most of their experience and prepare for their new lives.

4:00 Relax in the new quarters

6:00 Dinner in the room

7:00 Meet the other guests from a distance

8:00 Early Bedtime

Monday - Thursday

7:00 Breakfast

8:00 Relax in a sunbeam

9:00 Hop about aerobics

10:00 Bunny deep breathing and relaxation exercises

11:00 Mediations on a carrot

12:00 Noon repast

1:00 Short rest

2:00 "Shredding as a stress reducer"

3:00 "Compost production and you"

4:00 "Stand tall stretching to obtain new levels on understanding"

5:00 "Live close to the earth buffet"

6:00 Vegetarian dinner

7:00 Social discussion with other attendees

8:00 Bedtime

Friday will be a travel day with a trip to Scranton, an overnight stay at a road side bunny inn and then the final journey to the forever homes.

This morning my bunnies informed me they are getting me a new recliner or sofa (my choice) for the living room. However, they need me to drive them to the store to pick it out and it seems that furniture stores don't take BunnyExpress cards so they might need a loan to pay for it. Is having bunnies really so different than having children?

In order to renovate the garage which holds all the foster bunnies, everyone was sent to the shelter for a week of "Bunny Camp."

The tough part about sending a dozen bunnies to "Bunny Camp" is getting all their gear packed. That is 72 little outfits, 12 sleeping bags, 12 bathing suits, 24 towels, 24 washcloths and 12 kit bags. Or maybe it is a bale of hay, 50 pounds of bunny chow, 22 dishes, 11 litter boxes, 11 cages, and 400 pounds of wood stove pellets. It is either one or the other.

Just got a text from Frick and Frack from camp:

"We learned a new song last night. Starts out Dog goes Woof, Cat goes Meow... It doesn't have any bunnies in it. Don't people know we grumble?"

Annie-Laurie Hunter

I just found out that while at camp my bunnies learned the song, "Alive, Awake, Alert, and Ready to Hop." And overnight they taught it to the 9 bunnies that didn't go to camp. Just imagine 24 bunnies singing that song and hopping in their cages or around the house in unison.

The bunnies got apples for breakfast in honor of Rosh Hashanah. Being a loquacious crew, all had something to say:

Piper: Are these Macs? I likes Macs best.

Me: Yup, they're Macs.

Big Brown: If we had Granny Smiths would we have a sour year?

Akita: If we had Delicious apples we would have a gritty year.

Hershey: How come we don't get to have honey with our apples?

Emily: Why didn't you ask about dipping them in chocolate, Hershey?

Charlotte: Emily, you are too clever.

Mary: Do I really have to stay in this cage and listen to this prattle all day? I can't wait until my hip is healed.

Sophie: If we lived a bit east of here would we eat Romes

Fluffy: When in Rome…

Grainger: Don't even finish that!

Hope: Can I have banana?

This morning Grainger asked, "Did the bunnies in England and France that were raised to prevent starvation during WWII have bananas for breakfast?"

"No, not even the children who raised them had bananas to eat."

"Is it okay if I am glad I wasn't one of those bunnies?"

"Of course. And it is important that you spend a moment to recognize the difficult situation they were in and to honor the bunnies who gave their lives and the children who raised them to ensure their families survived."

"This banana tastes different now."

Frick: Happy St. Nicholas Day Mom.

Frack: How come St. Nicholas didn't bring us any presents?

Frick: I told you not to eat the carrot and hay Mom put out for his horse!

Frack: Sorry, I got hungry waiting.

Frick: Mary said that Hanukkah gifts don't depend on being good like Santa presents do.
Me: That's true, but I would hope that being good would be its own reward.
Frack: Well, maybe, but I think we lucked out being foster bunnies in a Jewish home. I don't think we have a chance of getting on the nice list now.

Frick: Mom, since you won't be here for Hanukkah can we light the menorah?
Me: Amanda will light the menorah but you can say the prayers. Have you learned the prayers?
Frick: Baruch Atah Adonai.
Frack: Ner Hanukkah.
Me: There is quite a bit in the middle that you're missing.
Frack: Our way gets us to the pretty candles faster.

I just received a text from Frick and Frack:
Frack: Mom, did u tell Amanda how to take care of us?
Me: Yes, Y?
Frick: We told her we r supposed to each get a carrot and she said we should share one.
Me: Yup. You know that you share a carrot.
Frack: Did u tell her that we aren't supposed to have the menorah in our cage and the she has to light the candles?
Me: Yes.
Frick: Oh, well. We can still tell her that we r each supposed to get a handful of Cheerios to play dreidel with.
Me: Let me know how that works for you two.

I just got a text from Frick and Frack: Amanda lit the Menorah for us and we said the prayers. She made us say the part about being thankful for being brought safety to this time of year again.

And?

Well, it is our 1st Hanukkah; but Mom, we are grateful that we are here.

I just received a text from Frick and Frack:

Mom, Amanda took Emily home with her because she wasn't eating her dinner.
Me: Yes, I know. Emily is just in a bit of a funk and she will be fine.
Frick and Frack: She was quiet today but we were sort of busy, and then we were worried when Amanda took her.
Me: Well, it looks like she just needs a little special care and she will be back to her normal happy self.
Frick and Frack: That's good news; um, can we have her dinner?

I just got a text from the bunnies:
Mom, we were playing dreidel but
Blackberry said it is "Nom" not "Nun" so
he ate all the Cheerios.

Just got a text from Frick and Frack:
Frick: Mom, don't we follow a vegan, whole food, raw food diet?
Me: Yes, Y?
Frack: How r we going 2 have latkes tonight?

Frick: Mom, Frack bit holes in my yarmulke.

Frack: I was making ear holes for you so it won't fall off.

Frick: Oh, thanks, that's much better. Never mind, Mom.

Frack: Happy Hanukkah!

Just got a text from the bunnies:

Frack: Fluffy said there is no Hanukkah Fairy, is that true?

Me: That is true; there is no Hanukkah Fairy. Y?

Frick: We want to ask for something for Hanukkah and we don't know who to ask.

Me: You can ask me. If I can get it for you, I will.

Frack: Well, that's the hard part, Mom. You take great care of us and we r really gr8ful that we got 2 come here.

Frick: Yeah, all that, Mom, but we saw lots of bunnies on Facebook that have families of their very own and, well, we want one 2.

Frack: Yeah, Mom, can we have a family of r own?

Me: How about if I put your request on Facebook and we see what happens?

Frick: Thanks, Mom.

Well, here it is. *"Frick and Frack are spayed sisters who came into the shelter as a neglect case in June. They are, as you can tell from their texts, playful, fun bunnies that would love to have a real fur-ever home together."*

Cashew was not impressed with the new smoke and carbon monoxide detector and fire extinguisher they got for Hanukkah.

"But bunnies can't use a fire extinguisher and we can't get out of our cages."

"But all of your cages are on wheels and this will let me know that you need help."

"You treat us like human children."

"No, I treat you like bunnies that are as precious as children. "

"Do human kids get smoke detectors for Hanukkah? "

"Hanukkah and Christmas are a great time for parents to give children smoke detectors for their bedrooms if they don't already have one. And it is a great time to talk about fire safety and how to use a fire extinguisher."

"I have mixed feelings about you being a home inspector; I'm glad you worry about our safety but toys and treats are more fun."

"How about I treat you to a glass of carrot juice?"

It was the last morning of Hanukkah and Frick and Frack were the last cage of bunnies to receive breakfast. As I said good morning and opened the cage to give them their banana, I saw a little red bag in the cage. "Happy Hanukkah, Mom. We all pooled our allowances and we have enough to buy you a new vacuum cleaner. But we didn't have a ride to pick it up so you have to get it. "I think I can handle that. Thank you."

Then I went inside to hear Sophie announce, "Perfect! We can really shed today. Mom won't mind."

Houdini and Dave are vacationing here this week so Houdini can continue with medical treatment while her family is on vacation. I just went out to serve dinner.

Houdini said, "I read that if you put up a stocking Santa Paws will come, but I don't know if it will work because we aren't at home."

I replied, "I guess we will have to wait and see but I am pretty sure that if he knows if you are good or bad, he must know where you are."

Everyone was fed and as I left the garage I heard Frack say, "Darn! We should have hung up stockings too. Now the stores are all closed."

Me: I see Santa Paws found you.

Houdini: Yeah, he brought us a slinky toy.

Frick and Frack: Mom, look, he brought toys for all of us.

Me: Wow, how did that happen?

Frick: We woke up when he opened our cage door. He said the spirit of giving is universal.

Then Frack whispered: We didn't tell him that we really like the spirit of receiving.

Frick: Mom, this year is almost over and we haven't found a family.
Frack: What's going to happen to us?
Me: Well, you will stay here until the shelter's bunny room is renovated; then you will go to the shelter and be seen by the public.
Frick: How come we can't go there now?
Me: The cages aren't big enough for the two of you. There is only room for 8 bunnies now, but that will grow to 12 bunnies after the renovation.
Frack: So, the bunny room will be bigger?
Me: No, we are just going to have half again as many larger cages.
Frick: Did they get a Tardis?

Frick: Mom, can we have a party for New Year's Eve?
Me: Sure. What do want at your party?
Frack: Carrots and apple cider and fruit salad with bananas and grapes in it.
Me: Anything else?
Frick: Can we all play outside in the snow at midnight?

Baxter Bunny

"It's too crowded in here! Can you move over?"

"I can't move over. Baxter's taking up too much room."

"Baxter don't hog the whole cage! You're a rabbit not a pig."

"Yeah, well, tell Camellia to get her ears out of my face."

"My ears are not in your face! Brambles can you move over? I need to use the corner."

"I need it after you."

"Hey look, Two Legs is coming."

"Oh good, maybe he'll fill the water dish you dumped over, you stupid Ash."

"It wasn't my fault. Baxter hopped on me and bit my ear."

"That's because Camellia bit my butt."

"Well I wouldn't have bit your butt if you hadn't jumped on my foot."

"Will you kits stop grumbling? I have heard enough grumbling to last me three litters. I can't wait until Two Legs gets you kits out of here and into your own cages."

"It's your fault that mom is mad."

"Is not."

"Hey, where am I going? Hey, Two Legs, put me down. Hey, where are you taking me? Mom!!! Two Legs has me." Baxter scrabbled to gain purchase against Two Leg's body. But old Two Legs held Baxter away from himself as he walked swiftly towards some carry bins. He put Baxter in the plastic bin and firmly closed the metal door. Baxter was only alone for a minute before he was joined by Camellia, then Snowdrop, Brambles, Bella, and finally Ash.

"Hey, where's Mom?"

"I don't know. Maybe she's still in the cage?"

They were looking around when Camellia called, "Hang on everyone, we're moving!"

"I don't like this," grumbled Snowdrop as the cage swung gently to and fro as the man lugged the pet carrier to the truck.

The six little bunnies curled up together for comfort as the man stowed the pet carrier in the bed of the pick-up truck, climbed in the cab and started the engine.

"What was that?" Snowdrop burrowed under Baxter and Brambles as the truck lurched into motion.

Ash looked through the vent holes and exclaimed, "The world is going really fast!"

"You are so dumb, Ash. The world isn't moving; we are!" said Camellia and Baxter together.

An hour later the truck stopped in a large parking lot and the man took the bunnies into a pet store.

"We can only take two today. Bunnies aren't

selling like they used to. The shelters and the rescues have been putting signs up telling everyone not to buy pet bunnies anymore. And the shelter is adopting them out already spayed and neutered."

"Fine. How about these two?" He pulled Snowdrop and Brambles out of the carrier. Then he collected his money and left the store.

"Freakin' House Rabbit Society. This used to be a decent business. Freakin' rabbit rescue people telling everyone not to buy bunnies and to spay and neuter. You spay and neuter all the bunnies and where do you think bunnies will come from? Maybe I can grow meat rabbits for Whole Foods." As he drove down the back road, Two Legs continued to rage until he stopped at a wide spot. He got out of truck, lifted the carrier down and opened the door at the edge of the road.

"Get the hell out of here. You aren't worth feeding."

Camellia, Baxter, Bella and Ash were sitting under the boughs of a pine that evening. Ash stood up to look around. "Look at those little purple flowers. I bet they would be tasty. What do you think purple tastes like?"

"Ash, purple is a color, not a taste."

"Well, I am going to taste the purple."

Bella was shivering with fear and excitement. "You shouldn't go out there. Remember what Mom said, 'Don't even go in a meadow at dusk.' And that is a meadow, I'm sure it is, and this is dusk."

"But they're purple."

"They will still be purple when it's dark," grumbled Baxter.

"No, they won't, they'll be black. I'm going to taste the purple."

Ash hopped into the meadow and nibbled a purple flower, "Purple tastes great!" he shouted back to his litter mates.

"Shhhh" chided Camellia.

"Come and taste the purple," yelled Ash and he jumped happily in the air and kicked his little heels.

He had barely landed when he was whisked into the air screaming, "OWWWWWWW!" His scream faded as he was flew across the meadow and out of sight.

Baxter watched in wide-eyed amazement, then whispered, "I always wondered why that bird was called an owl. I guess now we know."

"Do you think he will be alright?" whimpered Bella.

Camellia was getting over the shock of seeing her brother carried away. "I think that this meadow is no place for a dumb bunny. We need to be very careful."

"Let's think about the stories Mom told us about the wild bunnies. I think we are going to have to be like them." Baxter then hunkered down, low to the ground, and nibbled as he tried to think. What was that poem?

"Something overhead,

Stay near the edge,

A place to run from and a place to run to.

Zig Zag,

Zig Zag, around and back." Camellia recited the poem their mother recited each morning.

Bella quietly sang the nursery song their mother had sung to them nightly as they nursed. Camellia and Baxter joined in:

"Nibble here and nibble there,

Hide in the tall grass it's always near,

Nibble a pathway and keep it clear.

Nibble, nibble everywhere."

The three sat together under the boughs of the pine tree at the edge of the meadow and took turns sleeping during their first night away from their mother and the safety of their cramped wire-bottomed cage.

Baxter was awakened by Camellia. "Listen, I hear something rustling."

"Shhh"

They sat very quietly until the fox had passed them no more than 20 feet away. "He is very stinky."

"Yeah, but he didn't smell us."

"What are we going to do? We aren't designed to be out here in the wild; Bella is grey so that isn't so bad but I'm almost all white and you have big white patches. We really stick out."

"How about if we go back to the side of the road and maybe someone will see us and take us home?"

"Okay, but we need to watch out for other animals."

The three were sitting in the tall grass along the side of the road nibbling and watching as a fourth truck rambled down the dusty dirt road. The green truck went past them and then stopped a short ways up the road. A woman in a greenish grey uniform got out of the truck and walked slowly back down the road. She spotted the white of Camellia. "Well, what do we have here? You don't belong out here."

Mesmerized, the bunnies bolted at the last second. "Scatter!" called Baxter and three little bunnies ran in three directions. Baxter felt himself scooped up and cradled gently in the woman's arms. He struggled for a moment before settling. "You can't be more that 8 weeks old. You don't belong out here. Let me get you in a carrier and then I'll try to find your little friends."

She held Baxter as she arranged a towel at the bottom of a carrier and placed him inside. "I'll get you some food in a few minutes. Let me get your little friends."

Scanning the roadside, she spotted Camellia and Bella. She focused on Camellia and walked over to her. Bella watched the woman pick up Camellia. But at that moment, a feral cat pounced on Bella. Her scream caused the woman to turn, but it was too late. The cat had secured its lunch and sauntered away, thinking "Lunch to go."

The woman tucked Camellia into the carrier then searched the area for more little bunnies. After 15 minutes she returned to her truck and checked on her charges.

"Well, you two, let's get you some proper care."

Camellia and Baxter were placed in cages next to each other in a room with many other cages, each with a rabbit in it. The rabbit were all sizes, colors, and ages. "Wow, what is this place?"

Angel, a floppy eared, raggedy grey bunny in the cage next to Baxter said, "It's the shelter, kit. Aren't you kind of young to end up here? You should barely be out of your nest."

Baxter, who had never seen an old bunny before, stammered "I-I think we got lost. Two Legs took us in a rattley thing that made the world go fast and we went to a stinky place where two of our litter were dropped off and then he took us to a really big place and there were four of us but now we're here."

"Hey, kit, you know how to count?"

"Yes."

"Well, there's only two of you that I can see."

Baxter got very quiet and whispered, "Owl and Cat."

"Yeah, happens to the best of them. You just sit tight, kit. You'll be safe here. In a couple of months when you're old enough they'll take you in for a little adjustment and then you can find a nice family that will take you to a home."

"Have you ever been to a home?"

"Yeah, I had a girl to take care of me. I had her well trained too. Banana in the morning, green fluffy hay, salad every night, fresh water every time she came into the room. Yup, I had her trained."

"Why are you here?"

"She got a boyfriend and stopped taking care of

me. Her mother said she outgrew me, so here I am, an old bunny with a sore foot and not much hop left in me, sitting around this place."

The bunny in the cage next to Angel called out, "Angel, you need to stop feeling sorry for yourself."

"I know, Blueberry, but I miss my girl."

"Ah, forget about her, you gots to look to the future. Me, I am going to find me a man that wants a cool bunny like me. He'll climb on the floor with me and I will hop all over him. He won't even care if I leave a coco puff or two around. Yup, I am going to find me a real man."

Camellia, who had been quietly listening and looking around at the many cages asked, "How long do we have to stay here? Can we just go home? I think our mom is missing us."

Sage, eating hay in the cage next to Camellia, said, "Sorry honey, you are going to be here for a while so you may as well get used to it. But it's okay: we have this room to ourselves, except for when the people come in. And if you like the person, you just go right up to the front of your cage and stick your nose out like this." Sage demonstrated sticking her nose out through the bars of the cage, standing up tall and hopping from one side of the cage to the other. "If you don't like the person then just turn around and show them your butt."

"The rest of the time it is just us bunnies and we have plenty of fun. So, you just don't worry. You're safe now and at least here we are warm and have food and room service."

Camellia hopped over to the side of her cage and whispered to Baxter, "This may be safe and I have lots of room in my cage and no one is dumping over the water bowl or biting me in the butt, but my heart hurts."

Frick: Mom, where are the Wonder Bread bags?
Me: Why are you looking for Wonder Bread bags?
Frack: So we can put on our boots and come help you shovel.
Me: I just finished shoveling.
Frick: Then can we go out and play in the snow?
Me: Sure, just as soon as you find the Wonder Bread bags.

Frick and Frack were ready when I served breakfast this morning.
Frick: Mom we have been reading about bunny nutrition.
Frack: From now on we only want to eat a little bit of fresh fruit, we want fresh greens every day, and we are going to have 90% of our diet from hay.
Frick: And we aren't going to have any store-bought treats, especially yogurt drops.
Me: How is that different from what you have been eating since you got here?
Frick and Frack looked at each other. We'll get back to you on that.

It was an early breakfast this morning but that didn't stop Frick and Frack.
Frick: Mom, we are only going to eat raw foods and whole foods.
Me: Okay...
Frack: But, Mommm!
Me: What?
Frick: We want to eat whole foods and you only gave us a piece of the banana.

Me: Frick and Frack, when I was putting the Bunny Nutrition book away I noticed that there are numerous nibble marks throughout the book...

Frick: It wasn't me, mom: it was Frack.

Frack: I'm sorry, Mom; I was just trying to digest all the information.

Frick: How come you haven't bought us 3rd cut hay?
Me: It doesn't grow locally; our growing season is too short
Frack: Yeah, we know, the earth on its axis and all that stuff...
Frick: Is it important to buy local foods?
Me: I buy local foods for you whenever I can; it supports the local economy and is better for the ecology.
Frack: So, can we visit the local banana farm?

Frick: Mom, what kind of apples are these?
Me: Some of you have Empire and some of you have Macintosh.
Frack: Are they locally grown?
Frick: Do they have Listerine?
Me: Yes, they are locally grown, and no, they don't have listeria.

Frick: Mom, can we have daily brush outs?
Frack: And have our nails painted when we have our mani-pedi's?
Me: You hate brush outs and you would look silly with colored nails.
Frick: But Mom!
Me: Why the desire to change lately?
Frack: We want to find a family.
Frick: We figured that if we changed, someone would want us...
Me: If you need to change for someone to want you, it isn't you they want...

Frick: Mom, where's my snow suit?
Me: In your cage?
Frick: I can't find it. Will you help me look?
Me: Look in the mirror.
Frick: Why?
Me: You are wearing a fur coat!

Frack: Mom, I think we finished reading the Bunny Nutrition book.

Frick: We just have one question:

Frack: How would our lives be different if we went gluten free?

Me: I wouldn't give you any Fruit Loops.

Frick: You don't give us any Fruit Loops now.

Perry was a very sweet older bunny who literally found himself out in the cold. He was abandoned and found near a convenience store. A very nice person took him to the shelter where he spent some time hanging out and getting neutered. Perry was having a problem with his tear ducts so he moved to foster care. He went to the bunny ophthalmologist and dealt well with his treatments. Possibly because Perry was neutered so late in his life, he was confused about the purpose of furniture in his cage. He used the cage floor as a litter box and a litter box as a bed. Knowing that, his cage floor was covered in litter and the litter box had a nice lamb's wool lining. These are a series of letters that Perry sent to Bob, the shelter liaison at the time.

Perry passed away quietly in his sleep about a month after his last note.

Hi Bob,

Perry, the bunny, here. Annie-Laurie took me to the eye doctor. Dr. B. he shone some lights in my eyes and then put drops in my eyes and then monkeyed around with my tear ducts. He cleaned them out and I do feel a bit better. Annie-Laurie brought me to her house and said I can stay here at least until I go back to Dr. B. on the 11th. He'll try to clean out my tear ducts again. I'm trying to be brave about it. Annie-Laurie's going to the store and getting some new eye drops for me. I hope they don't sting.

Anyway, I wanted you to know where I am in case you need me for anything. I'm going to go have some lunch and take a nap. It was a tough morning.

Perry

Hey Bob,

Perry here (hare), I was startin' to think you were going to have to bail me out of this place today. First, Annie-Laurie brought breakfast late. I was sitting there starving until she moseys on down at 8:30. I could have had the back forty nibbled by 8:30 in the morning! So, she brings me some apple and fills the chow bowl and gets me some fresh water but she forgot the oats. You can't get good help these days.

After breakfast she comes back and decides it's face-washing time. She's big on face-washing time. She put me on the washing machine and dag-gonnit if the thing ain't moving. It was like I was in a cheap hotel with them vibratin' beds. Actually it was kind of nice once you get past the shock of the world moving under your paws. So we gets face-washing done and then it's time for maid service to clean the room.

She goes and strips my room and tells me that the bed is supposed to be the toilet and chides me for peeing on the floor. Now I don't know about you, but I am not going to pee in my bed. So, she tries to give me another bed but I told her that wasn't what I wanted. So after we went 'round a few times she finally got me a king-sized bed to sleep in with a soft lamb's wool comforter and she puts the toilet over in the other corner.

Then she tried to buy me off with a carrot. Well, I told her I can't be bought but I took the carrot and tested out the new bed and I reckon I'll hang out here a while longer.

She says I am drinking way too much water. I told her that if she don't like how *much water I drink, she should give me the hard stuff. She said okay and went and got a bowl of red stuff. She says it's called Pedialyte and maybe my salts ain't right. Yeah, I'll let you know about my salts, I thinks to myself. But it does taste pretty good.*

So, mostly it's okay here. I get a couple of bowls of food a day- the rule is that if you empty the bowl, she refills it. And I get some fruit for breakfast and sometimes oats and then there is a big salad for dinner and there is always hay to munch. So the food is okay and there ain't no barking dogs, so that's good.

At least I'm not the bunny in the corral down below. She had to have her butt washed. Bad enough I have to have my face washed every day, At least I don't have some schoolmarm washing my butt.

Hope all is going well for you. Say howdy to the crew at the shelter for me.

Perry

Hi Bob,

What a day!!! The eye doctor roto-rootered my tear ducts again. The stuff still didn't come out my nose like they hoped but at least it was all clear "saline" they call it this time. I get eye drops twice a day and Annie-Laurie will call him in a month about how I'm doing. I hope I'm doing okay because I don't want to do that again. Did you ever just want to bite someone's hand? Yeah, well, I didn't do it but I was thinking about it. I'm glad to be back here.

I'm not sure if I should hang out here or go back to the shelter. Here's fine with me, Annie-Laurie gives me good grub and it's quiet. I kind of miss visiting with you though. So let me know what you think.

Perry

Hey Bob,

Have you ever had a pear? I am thinking maybe I should change my name to Peary- ha ha ha. Someone just sent me note saying my name was Periwinkle. I wrote back that I haven't got winkle in me. I am glad you shortened it when you wrote to Annie-Laurie about me. That woulda been a tough one to live down around here.

I'm gonna need a larger waistband if I stay here too long though. That Annie-Laurie makes one mean apple. She makes a pretty good banana too. Abbey said she even had something called a grape one day. I am not sure what a grape is, but if is anything like a pear, I am just going to sit here and wait for it.

Perry

Hi Bob,

Perry here. Just wanted to say hi. My eyes are doing really well now. My face is getting fluffy again. It has been a long time since it was fluffy. I'm just hanging out here waiting for the elusive grape to show up. I asked Annie-Laurie about those grapes Abbey was talking about. Annie-Laurie said that I'm going to have to wait a while for them because right now they're costing two paws and a tail. I still fit in my hutch but my haunches are getting bigger. Annie-Laurie says that I'm filling out my fur suit very nicely.

Let me know if you want to get together for a visit. We can share some carrot juice and check out the does or something. We got a cute little one moved in next door- her name is Alyssum. Tarragon keeps hitting *on her but if I was given to chance, I would take a young thing like that into my hutch.*

Perry

Frick just said, "My nose looks pointy. Why is my nose pointy?"
Frack responded, "It is from sticking your nose through the bars, silly."

Frack: Mom, how come you don't let us help with the snow blower?

Me: It's a 5 horse power snow blower and you are only 2 bunny powered.

Frick: Oh... Can you get us a 2 carpet pony powered snow blower?

Me: There is a shovel, right over there...

Frack: Look at this yummy hay...

Frack: Mom, I like this Seek and Find book.
Me: That's "*Algebra for the Logarithmic Lagomorph.*" Why did you think it was a Seek and Find book?
Frack: It keeps telling me to find x.

Frack: Mom, are you sure this book knows its stuff?
Me: What book do you have now?
Frack: "*Geometry for the Logarithmic Lagomorph.*"
Me: That should be accurate, why?
Frack: It says corners are hot but ours are the same temperature as the rest of our cage.
Me: What? Where?
Frack: Here; it says the corner is 90 degrees.

Frick: Mom, it's snowing outside. May we have some hot apple cider?
Me: But you haven't been outside.
Frack: So...

Frick: Hey Mom, according to this book you are a bunny.

Me: What? I am a person, you are a bunny.

Frick opened the book and started with: Do bunnies eat carrots?

Me: Yes

Frick: Do you eat carrots?

Me: Yes

Frick: See? That proves it: you are a bunny!

Me: What book are you reading?

Frick: *"Logic for Lagomorphs."*

Me: Well, that might explain it, but I think you missed something in your syllogism.

Frick: Well, I did hop around.

Frack: I think she just has a sillyism.

While tucking the bunnies in tonight.
Frack: Mom, did we have a bunny mom?
Me: Of course you did. All bunnies have bunny mommies when they are very little.
Frick: I remember our mom used to sing to us like Louisa sings to her babies:
Me: What song does she sing?
Frick and Frack together:

> *Nibble here and nibble there,*
> *Hide in the tall grass it's always near,*
> *Nibble a pathway and keep it clear.*
> *Nibble, nibble everywhere.*

Frack: I remember the song and listening to Louisa sing it makes me happy inside.
Me: Then I will sing it to you also.

I just came home from the grocery store to hear a rhythmic thumping in the garage.
Me: Hey, what's going on out here?
Frack: Hi Mom, we're practicing.
Me: Practicing?
Frick: We want to be ready to do "The Cup Song" next year for half time at the puppy bowl.
Me: Carry on.
And the current 29 bunnies started thumping in unison, banging their dishes, and singing, "I got a ticket..."

Frick: Mom, you did a great job with the snow blower.

Frack: You look cold.

Me: Thanks and I am cold.

Frick: You should have some hot apple cider.

Me: Are you going to heat it up while I get changed?

Frick: We aren't so good with the microwave and you won't let us use the stove.

Frack: But we could share it with you when you have it ready.

Me: You bunnies all look so tired this morning, what's going on?

Frick: Mom, you know that song you sing us before you turn out the light?

Frack: The one that says, "Rest your head, close your eyes, and let your ears hang down low."

Me: The bunny lullaby, yes...

Frick: Well, we short up-eared bunnies can't droop our ears.

Frack: We stayed up all night trying and the droopy and loppity eared bunnies kept giving us advice, but we can't do it.

Me: Did you try laying on your side?

Frick: Mom, I've been thinking about apples...
Me: What about apples?
Frick: Well, there are a lot of kinds of apples and some are named for where they are from, like Rome and Cortland, and some are named for how they taste, like Delicious, but there isn't an apple named Newton; you know why?
Me: I am almost afraid to ask.
Frick: They fall off the trees before they can be picked.

Frick: Hey, Frack where did you go?

Frack: I had to go see the vet. Mom says my head's not on straight.

Frick: And she sent you to the vet for that?

Frick: Mom, I was reading about E. Cuniculi, you know the thing that Frack has...
Me: Did you learn anything interesting?
Frick: Well, I am not happy that she can't be cured and that she might get sick again from it.
Me: I'm not happy about that either. EC is a horrible disease that used to kill lots of bunnies but now at least we have treatments.

Frick: Yeah, about that. It says the E. Cuniculi is a protozoa.
Me: That's right...
Frick: So, is the medication an antitozoa?

Frick: Mom, Frack's head is more crooked.

Me: Frack, how do you feel?

Frack: How come everything is tilted if I am taking my medicine?

Me: We caught you being sick very early and sometimes things get worse before they get better.

Frack: Am I going to get better?

Me: I have every reason to believe that you will get better.

Frack: Can I still get adopted?

Me: Yes, but you will only be adopted to a family that understands that you have been sick and are able to take good care of you.

Frack: Are there people like that?

Me: Yes, Frack, there are wonderful giving people out there.

Frick: Mom, do you love all of us?

Me: Yes, why?

Hershey: You are really excited that we are leaving.

Me: I am very excited that you are moving one step closer to finding real homes.

Frack: Do you love me?

Me: Yes, Frack, I love you.

Frack: But you aren't sending me to the shelter to find a home.

Me: You were just sick and I want to keep you here with me for a little while longer. But you will get to go to the shelter for your book signing.

Frack: Love is complicated.

Frack: Mom, did you go to the feed store today?

Me: Yup, I got 2 bales of second cut hay and 100 pounds of bunny chow.

Frack: Well, you bought food for us but I am still mad at you for giving me medication.

Me: I know, but I did get you a special treat; I got some red clover for you.

Frack: Okay, I'll have some red clover, but I'm still mad at you.

Frick: Mom, we want to watch <u>Hop</u> for movie night.

Me: That's fine. I think the little bunnies will like that.

Frack: Can we have snacks?

Me: Sure, what would you like?

Frick: Kale chips!

Frack: Apple cider!

Casper: Baby carrots, please.

Butterscotch: May I have some red clover?

Buddy: Do we have any escarole?

Piper: I would like apple sticks, please.

Emily: I want kale chips.

Buttons: Just some carrot juice for me.

Patience: Apple cider and banana chips…

Fortitude: Oh, I would love some banana chips and maybe some blueberries.

Skyler: Do we have any meadow hay?

There is a reason we don't have movie night very often.

Frick: Mom, are we still in trouble?

Me: Do you think you should still be in trouble?

Frack: We didn't mean for the carrot we were roasting on the heater to catch on fire.

Me: And what would have happened if we didn't have a smoke detector to wake me up?

Frick: Okay, no more roasted carrots until summer.

Frack: Mom, Frick isn't moving.

Me: I know, sweetie. Frick got sick this morning with E. Cuniculi and Frick isn't going to move again.

Frack: It won't be the same…

Me: No, it won't. You were sisters and good friends.

Frack: People always said Frick's name first. Without Frick will people think that I fart a lot?

Me: Why would they think that?

Frack: Don't people Frack to get natural gas?

Frack: Mom, the girls in the cage next to me wouldn't settle down and go to sleep last night.

Me: Oh, Sunday through Wednesday they were being rambunctious?

Frack: They are always running around but I wanted to sleep.

Me: So what did you do?

Frack: I read them Peter Rabbit. It's what Frick would have done.

Me: Did it help?

Frack: The girls went to sleep and my heart hurts a little less.

Me: You've honored Frick. You're a very good bunny, Frack.

THIS I BELIEVE
By

Cauliflower the Bunny

I believe that life should be devoured. The world is a tasty treat waiting to be sampled. The carpets, the woodwork, the books, the cords--all are wonderful tastes and sensations. And the joy of hearing my name spoken and knowing that I am loved and adored for all that I do only enhances the pleasure of devouring life itself. Of course, carrots, lettuce, and grapes are wonderful too. But no one says my name when I eat them and I sort of like hearing my name.

I believe that it is important to enjoy the sunshine and the rain. There is nothing like getting drenched while being chased by my mom through a downpour and then being held and dried in a warm towel. But just lying in the sun and nibbling the grass around me is the ultimate in simple pleasures. My mom loves to hold me and smell my fur after I have been lying in the sun. She says I smell like sunshine itself. I like her to hold me.

I believe that one should always stop and smell the flowers before eating them. Oh, the sweetness of the flowers! The dandelions that covered the yard with their yellow blooms--alas they are no more. Now I am working on the clover with its pretty purple flowers that are so sweet and tasty.

I believe that barriers are put in

one's way by people who care in order to strengthen resolve and character. Barriers are challenges to be circumnavigated. If you can't dig under it or jump over it then just chew through it! No barrier should ever be allowed to hold one back from the adventures of life. Sometimes there are consequences for crossing barriers, but wounds heal and they are just part of the lesson on being more careful next time.

I believe in living in the moment. The challenges of yesterday are over. Each day is a fresh start with fresh fruit, fresh water in the bowl, and new adventures. There is always something new to explore, something new to find, something new to taste and devour. Every day is different. And I believe in taking a bite out of each of them.

I believe that I am loveable and I want to be loved and held by someone who will love me forever. Despite being given up because of what I am, I have found a home. I have a family with whom I can share my life. I believe that there is a home somewhere in the world where each of us will be truly appreciated for who we are and for the joy of life that they are willing to share.

I am Cauliflower and I believe in joy.

Annie-Laurie Hunter

Tonight, after everyone had dinner and were dressed in their little fur pajamas for bed, I heard one of the bunnies start singing and the rest join in: "All night, all day, Angels watching over me, my Lord, ..." Sleep well little bunnies.

ABOUT THE AUTHOR

Annie-Laurie Hunter is a home inspector by trade who is foster parent for bunnies. She enjoys quilting and writing. This is her second published work.

Made in the USA
Middletown, DE
12 March 2015